BEYOND THE MYSTERY

A curious journey Of Discovery

By

Emmanuel Noble

TABLE OF CONTENT

26. Conclusion

Introduction: Setting the Stage

*The introduction of **"Beyond the Mystery"** serves as the stage-setter for the entire story. It's where readers are first introduced to the main character, Sarah, and the ordinary world she inhabits. It provides a glimpse into her life, her personality, and the circumstances that will lead her on a transformative journey.*

In this section, readers learn about Sarah's daily routine, her curiosity, and her yearning for something more in her life. It's a relatable beginning, where the character represents the reader's desire for adventure and discovery.

The introduction also plants the seed of mystery with the arrival of a letter. This mysterious letter, without a return address, ignites Sarah's curiosity and sets the plot in motion. It serves as the inciting incident that propels Sarah into the adventure of a lifetime.

Moreover, the introduction hints at the theme of the book—uncovering secrets and knowledge hidden in the past. It establishes the central mystery, the enigmatic map, and the ancient civilization that holds the key to a deeper understanding of the world.

*Overall, the introduction is designed to draw readers into the story by connecting them with Sarah's relatable character and sparking their curiosity with the promise of adventure and discovery. It's the opening chapter that invites readers to journey **"Beyond the Mystery"** and explore a world filled with secrets, wonder, and the potential for personal transformation.*

Chapter 1: The Mysterious Letter

In the beginning of our story, our main character, Sarah, receives a letter in the mail. This letter is mysterious because it has no return address, and she doesn't recognize the handwriting. The envelope is old and dusty, which makes her curious.

As she carefully opens the letter, she finds a short message inside. It says, "Come to the old library at midnight. Secrets await." This message leaves her puzzled. Why would someone want her to go to the library in the middle of the night? What secrets are they talking about?

Sarah, full of curiosity and a sense of adventure, decides to investigate this mysterious letter. She wonders who sent it and what kind of secrets are waiting for her at the old library. Little does she know that this letter is just the beginning of an extraordinary journey filled with mystery and wonder.

Chapter 2: A Curious Discovery

In this chapter, Sarah can't stop thinking about the mysterious letter she received. The idea of secrets and adventure fills her thoughts. One day, while cleaning out her attic, she stumbles upon an old, dusty book. As she opens it, a folded, yellowed map falls out.

This map is unlike any she has seen before. It's full of strange symbols, and there are markings that seem to point to a location. Sarah's curiosity gets the best of her, and she starts to connect the dots. The symbols on the map somehow remind her of the message from the mysterious letter.

Excitement courses through her as she begins to wonder if this map could be related to the secrets mentioned in the letter. With a determined spirit, she decides to embark on a journey to find out more about this map and its connection to the old library and the secrets that await her there.

In this chapter, we see Sarah's curiosity and determination grow as she takes her first step towards unraveling the mystery presented by the letter and the discovery of the map. This curious discovery sets the stage for the adventures to come.

Chapter 3: The Mysterious Map

In this chapter, Sarah continues her quest to understand the enigmatic map she found. With the map in her hands, she carefully examines it, noting the strange symbols and markings. She realizes that the map might hold the key to unraveling the secrets mentioned in the mysterious letter.

Sarah's first task is to decipher the symbols on the map. She spends hours researching and comparing the symbols to various books and resources. Slowly but surely, she begins to make sense of some of them. It becomes clear that this is no ordinary map; it's a map of a hidden place or treasure, filled with riddles and clues.

With newfound determination, Sarah sets out to decode the remaining symbols. She discovers that the map leads to a location deep in the woods, far from her home. The map, with its cryptic hints, becomes a puzzle she is determined to solve.

The enigmatic map has ignited a sense of adventure and purpose within Sarah. As she plans her journey to the mysterious location indicated on the map, she can't help but wonder about the secrets that lie ahead. This chapter is a turning point as Sarah's journey takes a more defined direction, filled with anticipation and intrigue.

Chapter 4: Let's go on a Journey

In this chapter, Sarah makes the decision to set off on her adventure to uncover the secrets hinted at by the enigmatic map. With a sense of excitement and a touch of nervousness, she prepares for her journey.

First, she gathers supplies: a backpack, a flashlight, some food, and a warm jacket. She knows she'll be traveling into the woods, and it's important to be prepared.

Sarah also reaches out to a few trusted friends to let them know about her journey. She explains the mysterious letter, the curious discovery of the map, and her desire to solve the puzzle. Some of her friends express concern, but they also offer their support.

As the sun begins to set, Sarah heads out into the woods. The forest is dark, and the only sound is the crunch of leaves under her feet. She realizes that she's embarking on a journey into the unknown, and the feeling is both thrilling and a little bit scary.

In this chapter, we see Sarah's determination and bravery as she takes her first steps into the adventure. She's on her way to the location marked on the map, and the mysteries that lie ahead become more real with each step she takes into the dark forest.

Chapter 5: Meet a Wise Guide

As Sarah ventures deeper into the forest, she begins to feel a bit lost. The trees seem to close in around her, and she starts to worry that she might have taken a wrong turn. Just when she's feeling the most uncertain, she hears a gentle voice calling out to her.

A figure emerges from the shadows – an elderly woman with kind eyes and a warm smile. She introduces herself as Emily, a wise guide who knows these woods like the back of her hand. Emily explains that she was once on a quest of her own, searching for answers and meaning.

Emily offers to help Sarah navigate the forest and decipher the map's clues. She points out the signs of nature and the landmarks that hold hidden knowledge. As they walk together, Emily shares stories of her own adventures and the lessons she's learned along the way.

Sarah is grateful for the unexpected encounter with Emily. She realizes that she doesn't have to face this journey alone, and she gains valuable insights from Emily's wisdom. With her newfound guide by her side, Sarah's quest becomes less daunting, and she begins to see that there is more to discover in the forest than she ever imagined.

In this chapter, the story takes a turn as Sarah meets a knowledgeable companion who will play a significant role in her journey. Emily's wisdom and guidance provide comfort and direction to Sarah, making the adventure ahead more manageable and meaningful.

Chapter 6: Uncovering Ancient Secrets

In this chapter, Sarah and her wise guide, Emily, continue their journey through the forest, following the clues on the enigmatic map. As they walk deeper into the woods, they come across a hidden cave entrance that seems to match the map's markings.

With Emily's encouragement, Sarah enters the cave with a mix of excitement and trepidation. The cave is dark, and Sarah uses her flashlight to navigate its winding passages. Inside, they discover ancient symbols etched into the walls, as well as mysterious artifacts that hint at a long-forgotten history.

As they explore deeper into the cave, they stumble upon a chamber filled with ancient scrolls and books. These texts hold knowledge and secrets that have been hidden away for centuries. Sarah and Emily carefully examine the scrolls, trying to decipher their contents.

Among the scrolls, they find references to a powerful and ancient civilization that once thrived in the area. These people were known for their wisdom and connection to the natural world. It becomes clear that the secrets Sarah and Emily are uncovering are tied to this civilization and their unique understanding of the world.

This chapter is a turning point in the story as Sarah and Emily begin to unravel the mystery and uncover the ancient secrets that the map and the cave hold. Their journey takes on a new significance as they realize that they are delving into the history of a remarkable civilization that held knowledge that could change the world as they know it.

Chapter 7: The Hidden Temple

In this chapter, Sarah and Emily continue their exploration of the cave and its ancient secrets. They come across a concealed passageway that leads them to a remarkable discovery—the entrance to a hidden temple.

The temple is like nothing Sarah has ever seen before. Its walls are adorned with intricate carvings and beautiful artwork that tell stories of the ancient civilization's wisdom and connection to the natural world. In the center of the temple stands a magnificent altar, surrounded by offerings and relics from the past.

As Sarah and Emily explore the temple, they uncover more scrolls and ancient texts, which provide deeper insights into the civilization's beliefs and practices. The texts reveal that the temple was a place of learning and enlightenment, where the people of that time sought to understand the mysteries of life and nature.

The temple holds a serene and almost magical atmosphere, and Sarah and Emily can't help but feel that they are on the brink of something extraordinary. The temple's secrets are slowly unfolding, and they are about to embark on a journey of knowledge and discovery that goes beyond their wildest dreams.

In this chapter, the hidden temple becomes a pivotal point in the story, where Sarah and Emily find themselves face-to-face with the ancient civilization's legacy and their pursuit of wisdom. The temple opens up new possibilities and questions, setting the stage for the next stage of their adventure.

Chapter 8: The Whispering Statues

Inside the hidden temple, Sarah and Emily encounter a breathtaking sight—whispering statues. These statues are unlike any they've ever seen; they are beautifully sculpted figures of the ancient civilization's wise leaders.

What makes these statues extraordinary is that they appear to be whispering secrets to each other. The intricate carvings show the figures leaning close, as if sharing knowledge in hushed tones. It's as if the very stones are alive with the stories of the past.

As Sarah and Emily approach the statues, they realize that the whispers are not mere carvings but a part of the temple's design. Each statue emits a soft, melodic sound that is harmonious and soothing. It feels as if the statues are trying to communicate something profound.

Driven by curiosity, Sarah and Emily try to decipher the meaning behind these whispering statues. They spend hours in the temple, listening to the whispers and studying the carvings, hoping to unlock the ancient wisdom that lies within.

This chapter adds a new layer of intrigue to the story as the whispering statues become a mysterious and enchanting part of the hidden temple. Sarah and Emily are drawn deeper into the secrets of the past, determined to understand the significance of the statues and the knowledge they may hold.

Chapter 9: A Clue from the Stars

Sarah and Emily, after their captivating encounter with the whispering statues, decide to take a break and step outside the hidden temple. As they emerge into the night, they notice something remarkable in the clear sky – a pattern of stars that seems to match the symbols on the enigmatic map.

The stars create a constellation that, when observed closely, resembles the same symbols Sarah had been deciphering. It's as if the night sky is providing them with a clue that aligns with their journey. The connection between the stars and the map is undeniable.

This celestial discovery excites Sarah and Emily, and they decide to spend the night studying the stars and making detailed notes about their alignment. They believe that these stars hold the key to uncovering more about the ancient civilization and the mysteries they're trying to unravel.

As they gaze up at the starry sky, Sarah and Emily begin to understand that their quest is intricately linked to the cosmos. The stars, it seems, have a role to play in guiding them toward the truth hidden within the ancient secrets they've uncovered.

In this chapter, the story takes a cosmic turn as Sarah and Emily find a clue in the stars that deepens their connection to the ancient civilization and the enigmatic map. The night sky becomes a part of their journey, and they're determined to decode the message written in the stars.

Chapter 10: Take a chance

As Sarah and Emily continue to study the stars, they notice a change in the forest around them. The air grows tense, and the sounds of the night become hushed. They sense that they are not alone.

Suddenly, dark figures emerge from the shadows. It's a group of individuals who seem determined to keep Sarah and Emily from uncovering the secrets of the ancient civilization. These mysterious figures are not friendly, and they are clearly a threat to our two adventurers.

Sarah and Emily must act quickly. With a combination of resourcefulness and the wisdom they've gathered on their journey, they attempt to evade the danger and protect the knowledge they've gained. It's a thrilling and intense moment in the story as they use their wits to stay one step ahead of their pursuers.

This chapter introduces a sense of urgency and danger to the narrative. Sarah and Emily's quest takes a perilous turn as they face unexpected adversaries who want to keep the ancient secrets hidden. It's a pivotal moment in their journey, testing their resolve and the strength of their bond as they fight to continue their pursuit of knowledge and truth.

Chapter 11: The Forgotten Manuscript

After narrowly escaping the danger they encountered in the previous chapter, Sarah and Emily find themselves in a hidden chamber within the temple. In this chamber, they discover a forgotten manuscript, hidden away from prying eyes for centuries.

The manuscript is written in an ancient script, and its pages are delicate and yellowed with age. As they carefully examine the manuscript, Sarah and Emily realize that it holds the key to unlocking even more of the ancient civilization's secrets.

The text reveals detailed information about the civilization's beliefs, their connection to the natural world, and their understanding of the cosmos. It also provides insights into the purpose of the temple and the significance of the whispering statues.

Sarah and Emily are filled with a sense of awe and wonder as they read the manuscript. It's as if they've stumbled upon a treasure trove of knowledge that has been lost to the world for far too long.

In this chapter, the forgotten manuscript becomes a crucial piece of the puzzle. Sarah and Emily now have access to a wealth of information that could help them decipher the remaining mysteries and complete their quest to uncover the secrets of the ancient civilization.

Chapter 12: The Puzzle of the Past

With the forgotten manuscript in their possession, Sarah and Emily delve deeper into its contents, hoping to find answers to the remaining mysteries. The manuscript contains intricate drawings and descriptions of various artifacts, including the enigmatic map, the whispering statues, and the hidden temple.

As they study the text and illustrations, Sarah and Emily begin to piece together the puzzle of the past. They learn about the rituals and ceremonies conducted by the ancient civilization within the temple, which were closely tied to their beliefs in harmony with nature and the stars.

The manuscript also hints at a final revelation, a culmination of their journey that would reveal the ultimate secret hidden by the civilization. It becomes clear that solving this puzzle of the past is the key to unlocking the final piece of knowledge and understanding the true purpose of the enigmatic map.

Sarah and Emily are excited by the progress they've made, but they also feel a sense of urgency to complete the puzzle and discover the civilization's ultimate secret before it's too late. Their adventure is now driven by a sense of purpose and the desire to uncover the ancient wisdom that has eluded the world for centuries.

Chapter 13: A Cryptic Riddle

As Sarah and Emily continue their quest to unravel the secrets of the ancient civilization, they come across a cryptic riddle in the forgotten manuscript. The riddle is written in a poetic and enigmatic style, and it suggests that the ultimate secret lies in a location known only to those who can decipher its hidden meaning.

The riddle is a puzzle that challenges Sarah and Emily's intellect and problem-solving abilities. It speaks of the stars, nature, and the passage of time. The cryptic message teases them with clues and hints, but the answer remains elusive.

Determined to solve the riddle, Sarah and Emily embark on a new phase of their journey. They consult the stars, explore the natural world around them, and study the ancient symbols in the temple, hoping to find the key to understanding the riddle.

This chapter adds a layer of complexity to their adventure as they grapple with a cryptic challenge that will test their knowledge, intuition, and determination. The riddle becomes a central focus, and they are determined to solve it and uncover the civilization's ultimate secret.

Chapter 14: The Journey Continues

As Sarah and Emily work diligently to decipher the cryptic riddle, they realize that the path to uncovering the ancient civilization's ultimate secret will be a long and challenging one. They understand that they must continue their journey beyond the hidden temple, seeking more clues and knowledge.

They decide to leave the temple behind and venture deeper into the forest, following the hints provided by the riddle. The journey takes them to new and unexplored places within the wilderness, where they encounter breathtaking landscapes, unusual wildlife, and natural phenomena.

Along the way, they meet new people who share their passion for knowledge and the mysteries of the ancient civilization. These chance encounters lead to valuable discussions and insights that help them in their quest.

The journey continues to be filled with adventure and discovery, as Sarah and Emily grow more determined to uncover the ultimate secret and unlock the hidden knowledge that has eluded the world for centuries. With each step they take, they come closer to the truth, making new friends and facing new challenges along the way.

Chapter 15: Trapped in a Labyrinth

As Sarah and Emily continue their journey, they follow the clues from the cryptic riddle into a dense and mysterious part of the forest. They soon find themselves in a labyrinthine thicket, where the trees seem to twist and turn in strange patterns, creating a confusing maze.

The labyrinth is a bewildering place, with paths that lead in multiple directions and no clear way out. As they venture deeper into the labyrinth, Sarah and Emily realize that they are trapped in a complex network of intertwining paths. The walls of the labyrinth are tall and thick, making it impossible to see what lies beyond.

With each turn they take, the labyrinth becomes more perplexing. They are faced with choices at every corner, unsure which path is the correct one. Frustration and fear start to set in as they worry about becoming hopelessly lost.

In this chapter, Sarah and Emily find themselves in a perilous situation as they navigate the labyrinth, desperately seeking an escape. The labyrinth becomes a metaphor for the challenges they face in their quest, where the path to uncovering the ancient secrets is filled with twists, turns, and uncertainty. It's a moment of tension and uncertainty in their adventure.

Chapter 16: Uncover the Truth

Trapped in the labyrinth, Sarah and Emily continue their search for a way out. They've been exploring its winding paths for what feels like hours, and frustration has given way to determination.

As they press forward, they notice a faint, shimmering light at the end of a particularly narrow passageway. With hope renewed, they make their way toward it. The light grows brighter, and soon they emerge into a hidden chamber within the labyrinth.

In the center of the chamber, they discover a remarkable sight—a pedestal with a glowing, ancient artifact. This artifact is the key to solving the cryptic riddle and unlocking the ultimate secret of the ancient civilization.

Sarah and Emily carefully examine the artifact, and they realize that it contains knowledge and wisdom that has been preserved for generations. With a sense of awe, they decipher the final clues and understand the true purpose of the civilization's rituals and beliefs.

This chapter marks a significant moment in the story as Sarah and Emily unveil the truth they've been seeking. The artifact in the labyrinth becomes the final piece of the puzzle, and they are on the verge of uncovering the ancient civilization's ultimate secret. Their determination and perseverance have led them to this critical point in their adventure.

Chapter 17: An unexpected Alliance

With the artifact in their possession and the ultimate secret of the ancient civilization now within their grasp, Sarah and Emily prepare to leave the labyrinth. As they retrace their steps, they encounter an unexpected presence—a mysterious figure who has been watching their journey.

This stranger reveals themselves as a surprising ally, someone who has been following their quest from a distance and who shares their passion for uncovering ancient mysteries. They introduce themselves as Alex, a historian and researcher with deep knowledge of the civilization they've been exploring.

Alex explains that they have been studying the same civilization for years and have made significant discoveries. They offer their expertise and insights to help Sarah and Emily unlock the full extent of the knowledge contained within the artifact and the ancient secrets they've uncovered.

With this newfound ally by their side, Sarah, Emily, and Alex form a strong and united team. Their shared knowledge and determination make them even more capable of understanding the wisdom of the civilization and how it can be shared with the world.

This chapter introduces a surprising twist as an unexpected ally joins their journey. Sarah and Emily are no longer alone in their quest to understand the ancient civilization's secrets. The addition of Alex adds depth and expertise to their group, making their mission even more compelling and meaningful.

Chapter 18: Face the forces of darkness

With their newfound ally, Alex, Sarah and Emily continue their quest to understand the ancient civilization's secrets. However, as they delve deeper into their research, they realize that there are dark forces at play—groups who seek to keep the knowledge hidden and who will stop at nothing to protect their secrets.

Sarah, Emily, and Alex become the target of these dark forces. They encounter obstacles and threats that test their resolve and determination. The dark forces will do anything to prevent the ancient wisdom from being revealed to the world.

As they face these challenges, the group must rely on their knowledge, resourcefulness, and the strong bond they've formed to protect themselves and the valuable knowledge they've uncovered. The battle against these dark forces becomes a central conflict in their journey.

In this chapter, the story takes a suspenseful turn as Sarah, Emily, and Alex confront the dangers that come with seeking the truth. The presence of dark forces adds tension and excitement to their adventure, as they are forced to defend the knowledge they've worked so hard to uncover.

Chapter 19: The Power of Friendship

Amid the challenges posed by the dark forces, Sarah, Emily, and Alex discover that their greatest strength lies in their friendship and mutual support. As the danger escalates, they realize that their bond has grown even stronger.

Facing adversity together, they learn to trust one another's skills and knowledge. They provide emotional support during moments of doubt and offer encouragement when the odds seem stacked against them. Through their friendship, they find the courage to persevere and continue their mission.

The power of friendship becomes a driving force in their quest to safeguard the ancient wisdom and share it with the world. Sarah, Emily, and Alex realize that their combined strength is what will ultimately allow them to overcome the dark forces and fulfill their mission.

This chapter highlights the importance of friendship and teamwork in the face of adversity. The bonds formed between the characters provide them with the resilience and determination needed to face the challenges ahead and succeed in their quest to preserve and share the ancient knowledge they've uncovered.

Chapter 20: The Final Fight

In this climactic chapter, Sarah, Emily, and Alex's relentless pursuit of the ancient civilization's secrets brings them face to face with the dark forces that have been pursuing them. The confrontation with these adversaries is inevitable, and the stakes are higher than ever.

The dark forces, determined to keep the ancient wisdom hidden, make their move to stop Sarah, Emily, and Alex. A tense standoff ensues, and a battle of wits and wills commences. The group faces obstacles and challenges as they strive to protect the knowledge they've worked so hard to uncover.

As the confrontation unfolds, the true nature of the dark forces' motives and their connection to the ancient civilization is revealed. The conflict is not merely about preserving the secrets but understanding the profound impact these secrets could have on the world.

In this chapter, the story reaches its climax as Sarah, Emily, and Alex engage in a final, high-stakes confrontation with the dark forces. The resolution of this conflict will determine whether the ancient knowledge remains hidden or is shared with the world, and the outcome will shape the course of their adventure.

Chapter 21: Restoring Balance

In the aftermath of the final confrontation with the dark forces, Sarah, Emily, and Alex emerge victorious. They have safeguarded the knowledge of the ancient civilization and have prevented it from falling into the wrong hands.

With the threat neutralized, the group is left to ponder the true purpose of the ancient wisdom they've uncovered. They realize that this knowledge has the potential to bring about positive change in the world. It can help restore balance and harmony between humanity and nature, just as the ancient civilization had intended.

Sarah, Emily, and Alex take it upon themselves to share the knowledge with the world, working together to create a plan to educate and inspire others. Their mission becomes one of restoration, using the ancient wisdom to guide humanity towards a more balanced and harmonious existence.

This chapter marks a turning point in the story as the characters recognize their responsibility to preserve and share the knowledge they've uncovered. Their journey is now focused on the greater good, and they are determined to use the wisdom of the ancient civilization to make a positive impact on the world.

Chapter 22: Lessons in the secrets

As Sarah, Emily, and Alex continue their mission to share the ancient wisdom they've uncovered, they realize that the journey itself has taught them valuable lessons.

They've learned the importance of curiosity and the pursuit of knowledge, even when faced with challenges and danger. They've discovered the strength that comes from friendship and teamwork, as well as the power of perseverance in the face of adversity.

The ancient civilization's secrets have taught them to appreciate the interconnectedness of humanity and the natural world, emphasizing the need to protect and preserve our environment. These lessons become a guiding light as they work to spread the knowledge they've gained.

In this chapter, the characters reflect on the profound impact their journey has had on their lives. The lessons they've learned from the mystery have become a source of inspiration and guidance, shaping their purpose as they strive to make the world a better place through the wisdom of the ancient civilization.

Chapter 23: Returning Home

Having fulfilled their mission to safeguard the ancient wisdom and share it with the world, Sarah, Emily, and Alex decide it's time to return home. They've journeyed through forests, discovered hidden temples, and faced dark forces, and now it's time to bring their adventure to a close.

Returning home is bittersweet for the group. They've experienced personal growth, forged lasting friendships, and made a meaningful impact on the world by preserving the ancient knowledge. Yet, they also look forward to the familiarity and comforts of home.

As they journey back, they carry with them the memories of their remarkable adventure, the lessons they've learned, and a sense of fulfillment in knowing they've made a difference. They are ready to share their experiences with others, hoping to inspire curiosity and a renewed appreciation for the mysteries of the past.

This chapter marks the end of their physical journey but the beginning of a new chapter in their lives. Returning home, they carry with them the wisdom of the ancient civilization and a sense of purpose that will continue to guide them in their future endeavors.

Chapter 24: Sharing the Adventure

Back home, Sarah, Emily, and Alex decide to document their incredible journey and the knowledge they've uncovered. They write books, create presentations, and share their experiences with the world through lectures and exhibitions.

They find that people are captivated by their story, and their mission to protect and share the ancient wisdom resonates with many. They inspire others to embark on their own adventures and to pursue knowledge and understanding.

Through sharing the adventure, they create a legacy that extends beyond their own experiences. They pass on the torch of curiosity and exploration, encouraging future generations to seek out mysteries and uncover the secrets of the past.

This chapter is a reflection of the impact Sarah, Emily, and Alex's adventure has on others. It underscores the importance of sharing knowledge and inspiring others to embark on their own quests for discovery and understanding.

Chapter 25: A New Beginning

With their mission to preserve and share the ancient wisdom a success, Sarah, Emily, and Alex embrace a new beginning. They continue their research and exploration, working on new projects and initiatives to further their mission of preserving knowledge and restoring balance.

Their friendship remains strong, and they are ready to face new challenges and embark on new adventures. They understand that the quest for knowledge is never-ending, and there are always more mysteries to unravel and more wisdom to be uncovered.

This final chapter represents the start of a new phase in their lives, full of possibilities and opportunities. They look forward to a future where they can make a lasting impact on the world, guided by the wisdom of the past and the strength of their friendship.

Chapter 26

Conclusion: Wrapping Up the Journey

*The conclusion of **"Beyond the Mystery"** serves as the final chapter in the book, wrapping up the intricate journey that the characters have undertaken. It's the culmination of the story, where the various plot threads and character arcs find resolution.*

In this section, readers witness the fulfillment of the main character's quest. After overcoming obstacles, discovering secrets, and facing adversaries, the characters have reached the end of their adventure. The ultimate secret of the ancient civilization, the purpose of the enigmatic map, and the wisdom they've uncovered now come together to form a comprehensive understanding.

The conclusion ties up loose ends, answers lingering questions, and brings a sense of closure to the story. It's where the characters have completed their mission, and the knowledge they've gained is shared with the world. This sharing of wisdom not only fulfills their mission but also symbolizes their personal growth and the positive impact they've made on society.

The characters' relationships and friendships are solidified in the conclusion. They've relied on each other, supported one another, and grown together throughout the journey. The bonds formed in the face of adversity and challenges are now stronger than ever, and their friendship endures beyond the adventure.

Ultimately, the conclusion is where the characters look forward to a new beginning. They recognize that their journey for knowledge is never truly over, and there are always more mysteries to uncover. The book ends on a note of optimism and a sense of infinite possibility, encouraging readers to embark on their adventures and pursue knowledge with a sense of wonder and curiosity.

*The conclusion of **"Beyond the Mystery"** is a satisfying ending that ties together the narrative's threads, reflects on the characters' growth, and leaves readers with a sense of fulfillment, hope, and inspiration.*

www.ingramcontent.com/pod-product-compliance
Lightning Source LLC
Chambersburg PA
CBHW071012260726

48661CB00007B/2918